D1074237

GUYS' GUIDES

The Real Deal

A Guy's Guide to Being a Guy

Jeremy Roberts

the rosen publishing group's
rosen central
new york

Published in 2000 by The Rosen Publishing Group, Inc.
29 East 21st Street, New York, NY 10010

First Edition

Library of Congress Cataloging-in-Publication Data

Roberts, Jeremy, 1956–
The real deal : a guy's guide to being a guy / Jeremy Roberts.—
1st ed.
p. cm.
Includes bibliographical references and index.
Summary: Discusses traditional, current, and stereotypical concepts of masculinity and provides advice for boys on how to deal with becoming a man.
ISBN 0-8239-3104-8
1. Men—Juvenile literature. 2. Masculinity—Juvenile literature.
3. Sex role—Juvenile literature. [1. Masculinity. 2. Sex role.
3. Identity.] I. Title.
HQ1090.R6 1999
305.31—dc21 99-40970
CIP

Manufactured in the United States of America

<<< contents >>>

About This Book

It's not easy being a guy these days. You're expected to be buff, studly, and masculine, but at the same time, you're supposed to be sensitive, thoughtful, and un-macho. And that's not all. You have to juggle all of this while you're wading through the shark-infested waters of middle school. So not only are you dealing with raging hormones, cliques, geeks, and body changes, but you're also supposed to figure out how to be a Good Guy. As if anyone is even sure what that means anyway. It's enough to make you wish for the caveman days, when guys just grunted and wrestled mammoths with their bare hands and stuff.

Being an adolescent is complicated. Take girls, for example. Just five minutes ago—or so it seems—they weren't much different from you and your buddies. Now, suddenly you can't keep your eyes off them, and other parts of your body have taken an interest too. Or maybe you're not interested in girls yet, and you're worried about when you will be. Then there's figuring out where you fit into the middle school world. Are you a jock, a brain, or what? And how come it seems that someone else gets to decide for you? What's up with that?

Yeah, it's tough. Still, you're a smart guy, and you'll figure it all out. That's not to say that we can't all use a hand. That's where this book comes in. It's sort of a cheat sheet for all the big tests that your middle school years throw at you. Use it to help you get through the amazing maze of your life—and to come out alive on the other side.

<<< Macho Men and Real Guys >>>

1

It's easy being a guy, right?

Sure—you were born that way. By definition, anything you do is a guy thing.

But some days it can feel a little trickier than that. Some days things

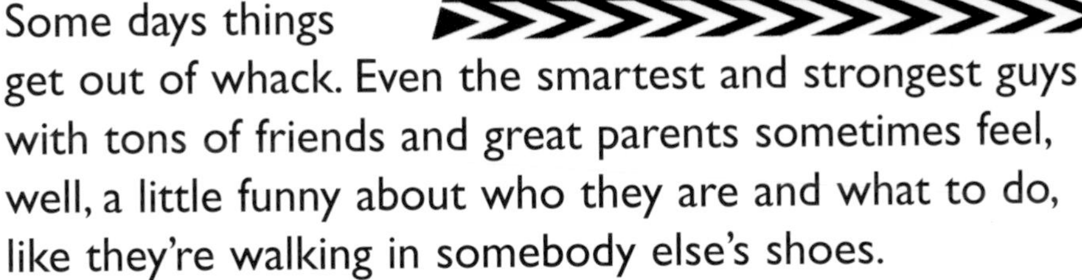

get out of whack. Even the smartest and strongest guys with tons of friends and great parents sometimes feel, well, a little funny about who they are and what to do, like they're walking in somebody else's shoes.

There are a lot of reasons for this. A big one is just the changes that guys' bodies go through as we grow. Becoming a teenager is like putting yourself through a hurricane—inside and out.

Then there's the fact that all of these changes mean huge possibilities. Today's guy has more to choose from in every way than his grandfather did. Having so much choice can actually be a little scary.

There's also the fact that society's idea of what it means to be a man—or a guy—is changing.

That's mostly good. Today's man can make a big difference to himself and the world just by being a man. He doesn't have to be locked into a job he hates. He can raise a family, have a lot of friends, and improve his community just by living there.

But life isn't all free pizza and potato chips. Many guys find that they're struggling against old ideas and misconceptions. Guys can be misjudged because they're small, because they're strong, because they're smart, because they're creative. There are a lot of myths out there about "guyhood." Sooner or later, you'll come up against them. You probably have already. Heck, you may even believe some of them.

>> Macho Myth <<

Ideas about what a guy should be like change all the time. Sometimes, those ideas get linked with certain images. They become stereotypes or even myths. Stereotypes are generalizations about entire groups of people. They become a false way of thinking about a person, even if they contain some truth.

You probably already know about racial stereotypes. And the odds are that you've learned about some sexual or gender stereotypes—for example, the one that girls can't play sports.

Guys are hurt by stereotypes like everyone else. Some stereotypes are pretty sly. They sneak up on us in weird ways.

For example, a lot of guys think that, no matter what happens to them, they have to be cool. They have to act like nothing bothers them.

Fail the biggest test of your life? *Ain't no thing. School's dumb.*

Girlfriend drops you? *She wasn't worth it.*

Parents divorced? *Better off without all that arguing and noise, believe me.*

All those answers come from the myth that guys are supposed to be invincible—Supermen—even if they wouldn't be caught dead wearing tights and a cape.

There's nothing wrong with being strong or with being brave. It's just that our view of what can be desirable can get pushed off track. Myths and stereotypes about what it means to be a guy are all over the place and they run deep. Many guys have been hurt trying to fit themselves into the distorted images of the "macho" man. It's kind of like trying to get on a pair of shoes that are five sizes too small. Even if you get them on, you aren't going very far.

A psychologist named William Pollack, who works with boys, summed up the common myths about men with four principles he calls "the boy code." Pollack says these are things that most guys take to extremes.

Here they are:

1. "The sturdy oak"—Men should be stoic, stable, and independent. They never need help in any way.

2. "Give 'em hell"—Men should be extremely daring, brave, and violent.

3. "The big wheel"—Men should dominate every situation, always be cool, and never be ashamed.

4. "No sissy stuff"—At all costs, men should not be like women in any way.

If you look at that list, you probably notice that most of the things on it are just exaggerations of goals that aren't

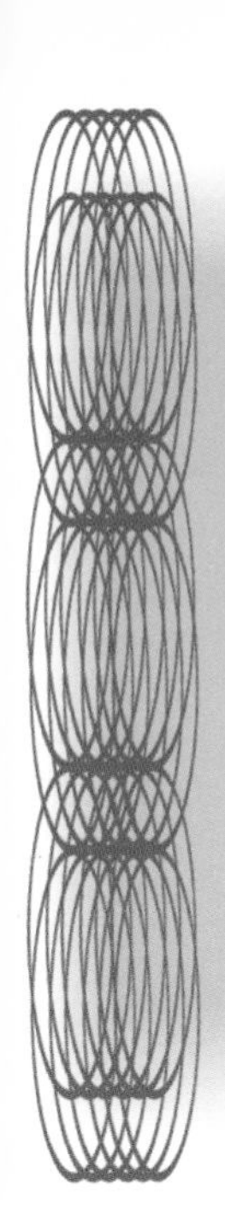

>> In a Word <<

Stoic.

Dictionary definition:

Indifferent to pleasure or pain.

Today's definition:

Part of the macho myth. Old thinking that keeps guys from being all they could be.

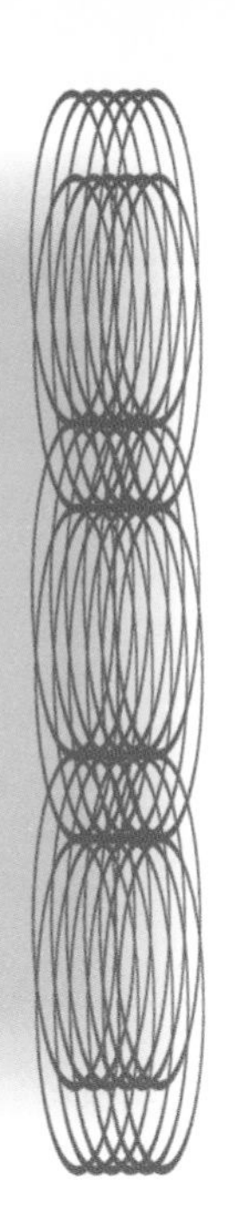

bad by themselves. It's good to be brave, right? But push it over the edge—be brave and independent always, no matter what, no matter where—and sooner or later, you fall.

You may have noticed something else when you looked at that list: You probably believe a couple of those things yourself, at least partly. And you definitely have acted as if you did. No sweat. We all do. Life is about where we're going more than where we've been. So stick around if you want to learn more about being a man without all the myths.

2 <<< Big Boys Do Cry >>>

Let's get this out of the way: Despite what you may have heard, BIG BOYS DO CRY.

And another thing: Guys have feelings. All of them. Guys feel angry, sad, happy, lousy, crazy. Always have, always will, despite what some people seem to believe.

Need proof? Most of the greatest love poems ever written were written by men. Check out the movie *Patton* to see a "tough guy" choking back tears. If you saw last year's World Series, NBA Championships, or Super Bowl, you saw a whole slew of guys jumping (and crying) for joy.

Let's be real about this. Being a guy does mean learning to control your emotions. Just because you're angry doesn't mean that you can break all the furniture in the living room—even if you always did hate that coffee table.

But the macho myth claims the only emotion a guy feels is anger. That's the only one he's allowed to show, preferably by blowing away the bad guys.

Nowadays, most people recognize that men do have emotions and they do show them. It's part of human nature. Of course, it's important not to be ruled by emotions. Guys have to balance it. They have to use their heads as well as their hearts. And they have to make their actions reflect that balance.

Emotion: It's A Guy Thing

Researchers have found that male infants actually express their emotions more than female infants. Parents and society curb this natural expression. By the time they reach school, many boys have been taught—wrongly—that boys shouldn't cry or feel sad.

>> Knights in Rusty Armor <<

But back to the teary stuff. Stereotypes change over time, which is one way we know they're false. That's true of the macho myth. Take crying. It hasn't always been that big a deal for a guy to shed a couple of tears. In fact, during the Middle Ages, a man was called a perfect knight only if he could cry. It showed he was emotional, which was considered a good thing. A truly great knight would go into battle, slay a hundred or so of his enemies, then bawl so much his armor would be in danger of rusting.

We're not living in the Middle Ages. There are definitely times when crying is going to get you laughed at or even in trouble. Some people, guys especially, still believe in the outdated macho myth. But don't let anyone tell you that guys don't have feelings.

It's okay to cry.

Period.

End of chapter.

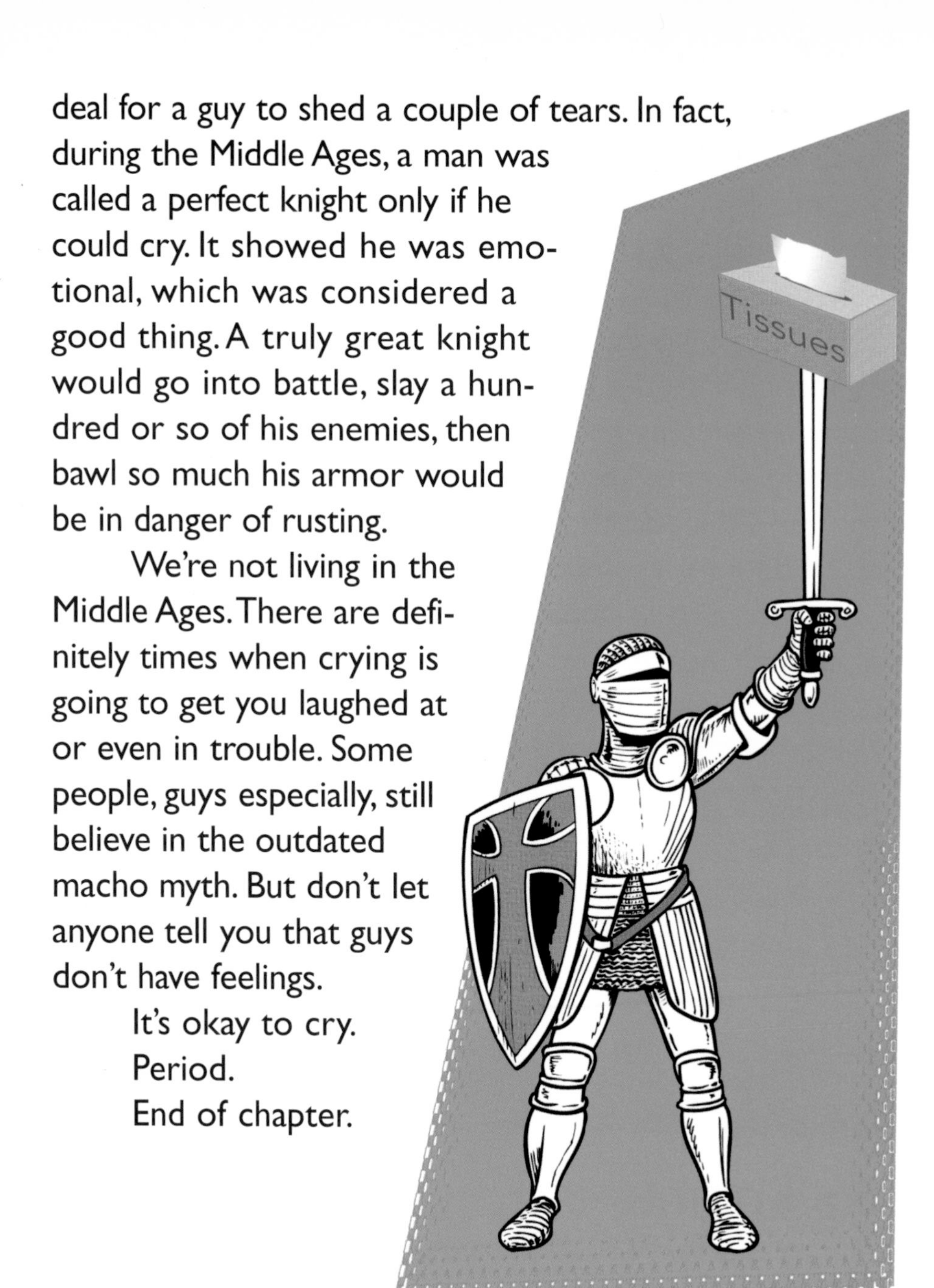

<<< Changes and Sex Myths >>> 3

Feel like you've got two left feet all of a sudden? Bumping into things? Dropping stuff? Could be a sign you're growing.

Sudden growth spurts are a serious guy thing. Some doctors even think kids literally grow overnight. But don't worry—you won't grow out of your pajamas, at least not all at once. Still, whether it's overnight or over a few years, growth spurts can change your sense of balance. Your body feels awkward because it's new. You haven't had quite enough practice ducking your head.

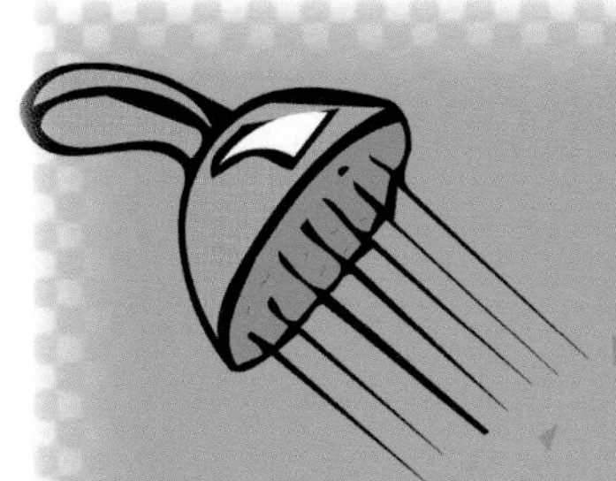

>> Peeeeeee-you <<

Among the many things that grow during puberty are your sweat glands.

So remember to shower, dude!

>> Changes<<

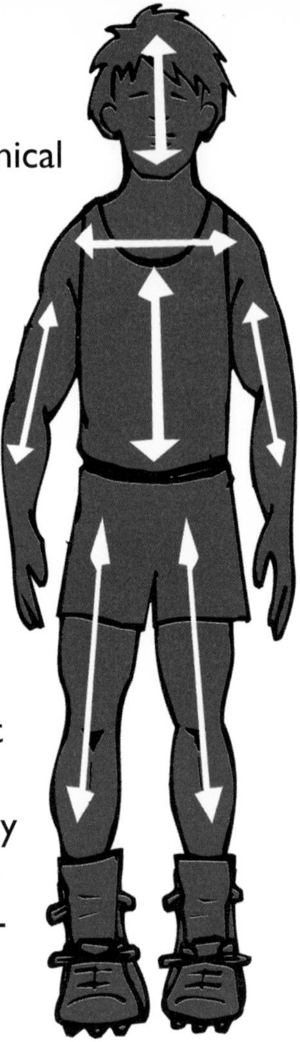

Let's pull out the spec sheet and get technical for a second. What exactly is going on with your body?

First of all, everything's getting bigger and longer. Your legs are stretching and your muscles are thickening. From the time you're ten until you're eighteen, your height will probably increase by about half. Your weight will more than double. You haven't grown so much since the first year you were born.

This massive growth spurt tends to emphasize differences in height and weight that weren't that noticeable before. It's important to remember that there's a very wide range of heights and weights. All are normal. All have advantages and disadvantages, even though they may not seem obvious to others—or to you.

Besides your arms and legs, your head is also growing. What's increasing is more than your hat size. You're becoming smarter in all sorts of ways. As a teenager, you clue in on abstract concepts and complicated relationships. You also are becoming a lot more creative. That can mean artistic. It can also mean seeing problems from a different angle.

And then there's sex.

Headline: Your penis is getting larger and your testes are producing sperm, just in case you haven't checked lately.

The word "puberty" is used to describe these changes. Puberty happens at different times and at a different pace for everybody. The average for guys is around thirteen, but puberty can also hit at around age ten and after age fifteen.

Zit City

It shows up the morning of the biggest day of your life—Killer Zit. It's so large it looks as if you've got a third eye. You think of wearing a bag over your head—except that the bag would have to be the size of Chicago to cover this monster.

First the good news: It will eventually go away.

More good news: Something like 90 percent of guys and 80 percent of girls get acne.

Now the bad news: That doesn't help you right now. And eventually isn't today.

There's no overnight cure. Acne is a very common problem and a good one to check on with a doctor or nurse. You can also try one of the acne medications at the drugstore. Most of these contain benzoyl peroxide. They fight bacteria and reduce skin oil. But they don't work for everyone, and they take time to work. In the meantime, try not to touch the offending blemish.

>> From Yuck to You <<

For the record, girls are going through similar changes.

This probably hasn't escaped your attention. Have you noticed, for instance, that they're not, well, "yucky" anymore?

You ain't seen nothin' yet. Girls' hormones are making their breasts develop. Their hormones also kick off the menstrual cycle, which makes reproduction possible. Like guys, girls go through puberty at all different times and at all different rates. They usually start out at least a year ahead of guys. It takes us a while to catch up. Some would argue that we never do.

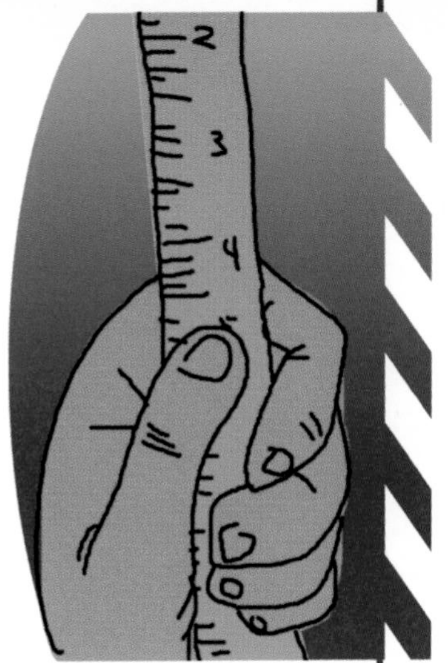

>> Size, Etc. <<

Every guy who goes through puberty becomes self-conscious about his body, and probably the number one body part he worries about is his penis.

Is it big enough? Is it a normal shape? Why does it keep popping up at the wrong moment? And what's with the wet dreams?

Every guy wonders about all that and more. The truth is that just like the other parts of your body, your penis goes through changes during puberty. But there is no "normal" size or shape for the male organ, and the shape doesn't have anything to do with sex drive or sexual pleasure. Neither does size. Nor will these factors make a difference when it comes to making babies. As for wet dreams (nocturnal emissions) and uncontrollable erections, those are a normal part of puberty too. Fortunately, they'll stop happening before too long.

>> Sex Myths <<

It would take an encyclopedia to detail all the myths about sex. Here's one of the biggies:

If you masturbate, ________.

Over the years, that blank has been filled in with everything from "you'll grow hair on your palms" to "your penis will fall off."

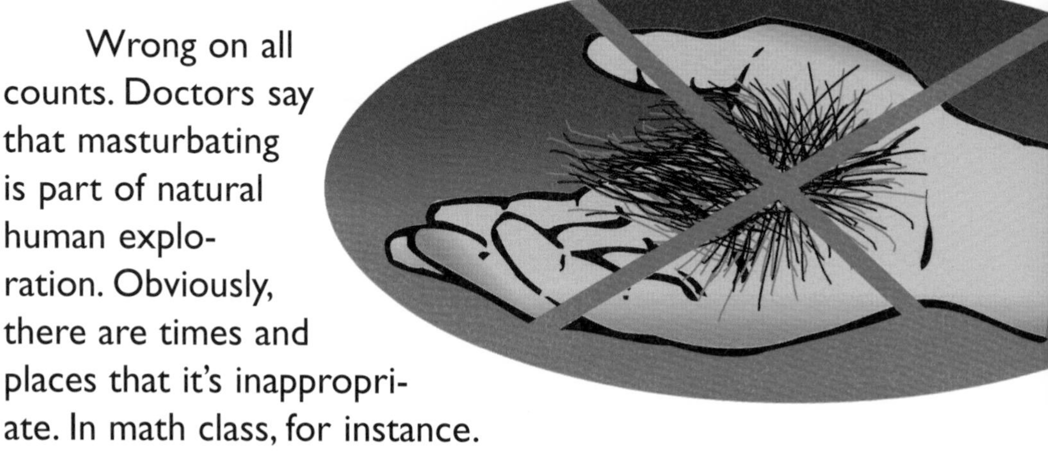

Wrong on all counts. Doctors say that masturbating is part of natural human exploration. Obviously, there are times and places that it's inappropriate. In math class, for instance.

Practically no one likes to talk about masturbating, but just about everybody does or did it at one time. It's no big deal.

>> Being Gay <<

Puberty kicks off a lot of sexual feelings and exploration. Among those feelings is an attraction toward girls.

And in some cases, an attraction toward other boys.

The exact nature of homosexuality—even how common it is—is a matter of intense debate. The latest research has led most scientists to conclude that human beings do not have a choice about their sexual preference. Experts believe it is programmed in by nature—kind of like your eye color. No one is entirely sure why one person is gay and another isn't. We do know, however, that talking about homosexuality doesn't make you gay.

We also know that a lot of people pick on others who are gay. They also use words like "queer" and "sissy" to put down other guys, no matter what sex they're attracted to. For some guys, anyone who doesn't live up to their idea of "macho" is weak and effeminate—queer.

They're totally wrong. First of all, there's a wide range of people who are homosexual. They may be fat, skinny, tall, short, well-built, strong, weak. Some have been war heroes. Some have been quiet accountants. Some have been macho-looking actors.

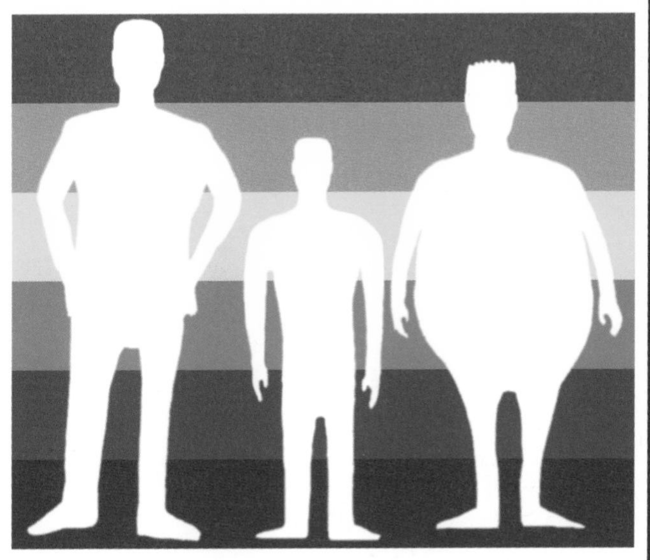

More important, most of the teasing happens because the teaser feels unsure about his own sexual identity. For him, the teasing is part of the process of sorting things out. That doesn't make it right. It's also not much comfort when you're on the receiving end. It's easy to say that being called a "fag" shouldn't hurt any more than being called a "jerk." Somehow, though, it often does.

How you handle it depends on the situation and your own style, of course. But whatever you do, no one has the right to put you down or attack you because of who you are or who they think you are. And it's okay to enlist the help of others, like guidance counselors at school, if you are constantly harassed.

>> Responsibility <<

Every guy has the responsibility to treat himself with respect. He also must treat others with respect. Not exactly a brain teaser, right? But it can be difficult when sex gets thrown into the equation.

Some guys forget that girls have to be shown respect. They push them around, ignore their opinions and concerns, and generally act like jerks. Part of that behavior is just being nervous about the sex thing. Part of it is following the lead of the wrong role models, whether from life, television, music, or whatever.

Everybody occasionally makes a mistake, guys included. But if you want respect, you have to treat others with it, too. That means remembering this golden rule: Girls who say "no" mean NO. Unwanted pinching, touching, wrestling, and even teasing not only show disrespect, they could potentially get you into trouble with the law.

>> Awkward <<

But most guys aren't trying to pick on girls or beat them up or disrespect them. They're just trying to figure them out.

Understanding the opposite sex is a lifelong process. It takes a lot of talking, as well as trial and error. It's important to remember that girls are going through a lot of changes, too. They're as confused as guys are. To make things worse, a lot of girls have been given wrong information about guys—just like guys have about girls. They may think someone who's an athlete is automatically a jerk, just because he's strong. Or they may think that a guy who's smart is boring and shy.

The only solution is to clue them in to real guys. Like you.

Spell It Out

Because men and women sometimes look at things differently, women and girls don't always understand when a guy is doing something because he loves her. For example, your mom might not realize that the reason you're hanging out in the kitchen with her one night is because you think she's special. You may have to put it in black and white for her by saying "I love you" out loud.

4 <<< Looking for Trouble—Not >>>

This ever happen to you?

You're sitting in the lunchroom, minding your own business, trying to figure out why the chicken chow mein smells like a little kid's sneakers. All of a sudden, some jerk announces you're sitting in his spot.

You're tempted to heave the lunch tray in his face. But then you notice he's a foot taller and fifty pounds heavier than you. His shoulders are wide enough to toss Steve Austin. And just in case you do get the drop on him, the vice principal is standing against the wall. He's squinting like he's trying to remember your parents' phone number. Naturally, the girl you've been trying to impress for weeks is sitting right at the next table, taking it all in.

Never happen to you? Don't worry—it will. Maybe not that exact situation, but something similar.

>> Tough Spots <<

We all know that the right way to treat people is the way we would like to be treated. Nobody wants to be bullied in the cafeteria or on the schoolbus or anywhere else.

But we don't always practice what we preach. And there are times when bad stuff happens. When you're faced with tough choices—for example, picking between serious bodily injury and serious ego crushing—there aren't easy answers. But there are a few things that you should try to keep in mind as you face difficult situations:

1. Try to do what you think is best.

   That's right. Contrary to the macho myth, real men think before they act. Try asking yourself questions such as: What are the consequences of going ballistic? What would happen to me if I jumped through the window? What do I do after the fight ends?

2. As much as possible, treat others the way you would want to be treated: If you don't like being bullied, then you shouldn't bully someone else.

3. It's okay to ask for help.

One of the old myths about being a guy was that guys never ask for help.

Wrong. Even the mythmakers didn't buy that. Just check out one of those old Westerns. The sheriff was always pulling together a posse. Wyatt Earp didn't go to the O.K. Corral alone.

Some guys feel there's a difference between asking a pal to back you up and asking for an adult's help. There's a lot of truth in that. Too often, though, that keeps guys from getting the help they really need.

If you are being threatened with physical violence, the line has been crossed—you are entitled to serious adult assistance.

If the same person or groups of people are teasing you or picking on you all the time, that's another reason to ask for adult help.

If your problem affects a lot of people, or your health,

or someone else's health, that's another reason to look for adult assistance.

Getting help from adults doesn't mean that someone else will fight your battles for you. An adult could just give you an idea or a hint on how to handle things better. A lot of times that's all you need.

Once in a while, guys run into adults who are brain dead. They don't understand what's going on. They may even believe in the old macho myth themselves. If this happens, don't make their problem your problem. If the teacher you asked failed to help you, go to someone else—a guidance counselor, for example.

The Adult Blowoff

Has this ever happened to you?

You finally feel as though you trust adults enough to ask a serious question, maybe about sex or health or something really important. So you do. They get a funny look on their face and say, "Oh, you don't have to worry about that." Or, "That's not a problem." Then they change the subject.

They're not dissing you. They're just even more nervous about talking about it than you were.

Most adults learn to hide their emotions as they grow up. Unfortunately, that also makes them less likely to talk about a lot of stuff they should talk about. Even with people who are close to them, like their sons or patients or students.

It's not your problem, it's theirs. If you feel they're blowing you off, say so. And then tell them you know this can be tough to talk about, but you're willing to take a shot at it and you hope they will, too.

That may not get you an answer. It may not even get them to pay attention. But at least it puts them on notice to take you seriously. And it may help them grow a little.

There's one other "guy" rule for dealing with problems. It's not a rule so much as a reminder:

4. No human being has always made the right decision 100 percent of the time.

Okay, so you couldn't come up with a good comeback on the bus. Or you blew your best chance at a date. It's not the end of the world. You'll definitely do better next time, because now you have more experience.

>> Homeboys and Posses <<

Friends are an important part of growing up. They're definitely handy if you're getting picked on, but that's not all. Just hangin' with a friend or two can make a day feel important.

For some guys, friendship can be very difficult. There are times when it's hard to believe that anyone in his right mind would buddy up with you. At other times, it just happens naturally. All of a sudden you realize the kid you've been skateboarding with for the last three years is your best friend.

When you're making new friends, it helps to remember that most kids are actually much more shy than they seem. It's also easier to deal with cliques if you remember they're really just groups of people. Approach them one person at a time, and you may find yourself fitting in before you know it. Or maybe you're the type of person who isn't comfortable in groups and prefers to have just one or two close friends. That's fine too.

>> Bullies <<

Bullies can be a difficult part of growing up. There are a lot of different approaches you can take to dealing with them.

Some guys, faced with a difficult situation (like what went down in the lunchroom), might try to make it into a joke. And a lot of times, humor is a good weapon for dealing with any situation. But life can be a lot stickier than television. You can't cut to a commercial when things get tough.

Confronted by bullies, a lot of guys have found that standing up for themselves works—though sometimes only at the cost of some serious bruises.

Experts—and guys who have been picked on by bullies and survived—say the "trick" to dealing with bullies is not to look like you're weak. As you probably know, this can be tough. Bullies don't usually pick on people who are stronger than they are. But you don't have to beat them up, or even fight, to stand up to them. A shake of the head can say you know the guy is a jerk but not worth fighting. That can help show others that you have self-respect and are not somebody to pick on.

Bullies are a tough problem no matter what. Just don't let the macho myth keep you from solving it. It's okay to look for help in dealing with a bully. Physical violence is never okay—especially when it's happening to you.

<<< Workin' for a Livin' >>>

5

So how many times have you been asked, "What do you want to be when you grow up?" A hundred times? A thousand?

Bad news—it's an unwritten rule of the universe that you have to be asked at least ten million times. And that's before you get your first job.

Relax. Most of the people asking the "whatyagonnabe" question mean you no bodily harm. It's a way for adults to say, "Welcome to the club," without sounding cheesy.

Of course, sometimes you want a snappy comeback.

But you can also give a serious answer. As a matter of fact, you may be trying to answer the question yourself.

Welcome to the club.

>> Endless Possibilities <<

Guys today have literally thousands of jobs and careers to choose from. More are being invented every day. In fact, there's a good chance that the career you'll choose didn't exist twenty years ago. It may not even exist now.

Many jobs require college degrees and even advanced degrees. On average, those jobs will pay more than jobs that don't. But it's wrong to think jobs that don't require college degrees are bad, or that only stupid people do them. The fact is, nearly every occupation today requires more knowledge than it did fifty years ago.

Take car repair. Back when your dad was a kid, fixing a car was pretty simple. Check the carburetor, adjust the distributor timing, and you were on the road. Nowadays, most cars don't even have carburetors or distributors. They have fuel injectors and silicone chips. That doesn't mean that today's auto technicians are smarter than yesterday's mechanics. But they do use their brains at least as much as their brawn. And that's typical of all jobs, from construction to rocket science.

>> No More Male/Female Jobs <<

A lot of the big news over the last twenty or thirty years is that women have been getting jobs that used to be mostly men's. There are a lot more women doctors than when your grandfather was growing up, for example. It hasn't gotten as much notice, but men have also been entering fields where women once dominated—health care, for example. In the past, if you were a guy and you weren't a doctor, you weren't in medicine. Now men are choosing careers that we traditionally think of as women's work, like nursing.

There's still a stigma attached to some jobs that women have historically held. That means, basically, that some people think they're women's work. But that's just old-fashioned thinking. Just about any job you can think of—artist, chef, truck driver, lawyer, accountant, or whatever—is something that a guy like you can succeed at.

>> Getting There <<

But how do you get there? Guidance departments in school can help show what some of the choices are. As you get older, guidance counselors can help you make decisions and narrow the possibilities. And other adults, including parents and relatives, may be good resources.

Parents can give you good advice—but they can also pressure you into making decisions about jobs and careers that you don't agree with. This is a tough problem that a lot

of guys face. Often, fathers want their sons to follow in their footsteps, or to be something they wanted to be when they were young, but didn't get the chance to be. There's nothing wrong with being an engineer or a doctor or a truck driver like your dad—but only if you do it because you want to.

As much as possible, it's best to be honest and open with your parents when discussing jobs and your future. It's not always easy. Even if you can get someone your parents respect to act as a neutral advisor, going against your parents' wishes may be one of the toughest things to do. It may help to know that when the decision is made for good reasons, parents usually do come around.

>> Getting Ready <<

Okay, so a job is years away. You haven't a clue what you want to do. But you can still stockpile your weapons to make a good choice. Here's how:

1. Education is the key to the future. The more you know about a wide range of subjects, the better prepared you'll be. That means learning about all sorts

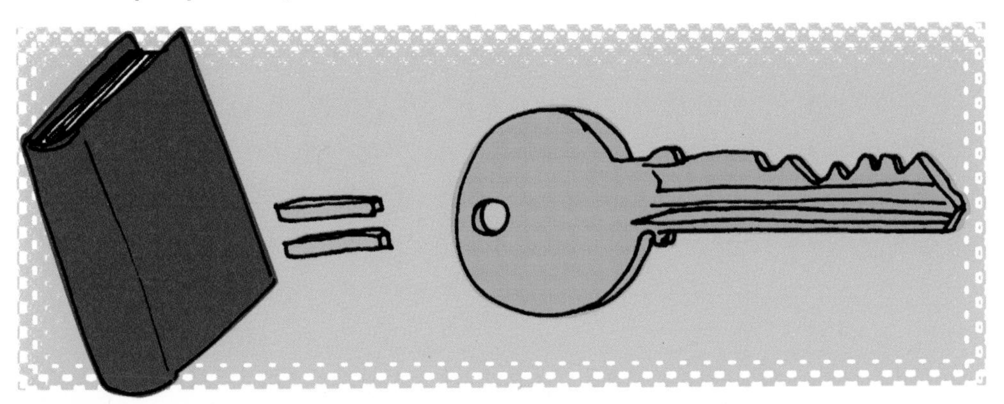

of stuff, and not just in school. In fact, the more you learn outside of school, the better. One way to set yourself apart from other people is by doing what you're doing right now—reading. It's the easiest way of gaining information.

2 Counselors and books can tell you about a career, but there's nothing like hearing it from the horse's mouth—or better yet, the farmer's or the cop's or the doctor's.

If you think you might be interested in being a teacher, for example, ask one what it's like. Some adults may think you're goofing with them at first. It's not every day that someone asks them about what they do. But most people will talk to you sincerely if they see that you're serious.

3 Follow your interests, and be creative about it. Like cars? Well, sure, you can be an auto mechanic. But you could also be an engineer, a designer of alternative fuel systems, or a planner for the first superhighway on Mars.

>> Beyond 9 to 5 <<

Guys have to remember that their job doesn't define who they are. It's important, but it's just part of the mix.

Society rewards hard work in all sorts of ways—money, fancy cars, big vacations. It's easy to get so caught up in work that everything else gets out of whack. But as guys get older, they realize they need to keep things balanced. It's important to support your family, but a family needs more than money to survive.

Beyond the family, a lot of guys find they need to connect to friends and the community. Adding something to the place you live not only helps others, but can help a guy grow. A lot of guys find that religious faith can be an important part of their lives. Everybody has a different style when it comes to religion. Some guys shout about it. Others are pretty quiet. Some more or less ignore it. It's important to work out your own take. Like everything else, it can grow and change as you do. Fortunately, a lot of other guys have walked this path before. Clergypeople and counselors are just some of the people who can offer hints and different perspectives on the role religious faith can play in a guy's life.

6 <<< Change the World —Be Yourself >>>

There was nothing very special about the store or the day. For that matter, there wasn't anything special about the four young men who sat at the counter of the Woolworth's in Greensboro, North Carolina. Except that, in 1960 in the South, blacks were not supposed to eat at a lunch counter reserved for whites. And the four teenagers who sat down at the small counter in the small store on February 1, 1960, were all black.

The waitress refused to serve them. They sat quietly at the counter from 4:30 PM until closing time, 5:30 PM.

The next day, they were joined by twenty of their friends. The day after that, more than sixty people came to sit at the Woolworth's counter where they were not served. The small protest against inequality had mushroomed. By the end of the month, other young men and women were staging similar protests at stores all across the country, even stores where blacks and whites were not kept apart.

These protests, led by guys not much older than you, helped change America. They were an important part of the civil rights movement. The young men who started the protests were Ezell Blair Jr., Franklin McCain, Joseph McNeil and David Richmond. Sometimes they're called the Greensboro Boys. They were so successful in their fight that today we don't even think twice about blacks and whites eating together.

At the time, though, it was a very brave thing to do. Other people—other young men, in fact—made fun of the protesters and harassed them. Some beat them and attacked them. Some protesters were killed. But other protesters stayed with it and changed America. The country is not perfect, but it's a much better place because of their efforts.

The Greensboro Boys didn't necessarily think of themselves as very special or very different before the demonstration. Truth is, they faced a lot of the same challenges you do. They were ordinary guys who knew that an injustice was being committed. They set out to change it.

Your background may be different from theirs. Your world certainly is. But you, too, can make a difference. Ordinary guys can do extraordinary things simply by standing up for what they believe in.

It doesn't have to be a big deal, either. In fact, most guys don't change the world in a way that the history books remember. Most guys change the world in very small ways—but ways that turn out to be very important to the people around them. That was how the "macho man" myth was destroyed in the first place. One by one, guys realized false images were making them wear shoes that were several sizes too small.

Value Yourself

Values are an important part of being a guy. Laws tell you what you can't do. Values tell you what you can and should do.

Building values is a lifelong process. Parents and religion aren't the only source of values, however. So are friends, teachers, and the other people around you.

>> A "True" Guy's Guy <<

Fred Rosen has what might be considered a "macho" job. He talks to murderers and writes books about them and their crimes. He's a writer of "true crime" books. You or your parents might even have read some of his books, which include *Lobster Boy* and *Gang Mom*.

You can't be a wimp if you're dealing with tough guys all day, right? You have to be at least as tough as they are. Most people probably think Rosen is a macho guy.

On the other hand, he spends his days caring for his baby daughter. He arranges his work schedule so he's there to feed her, bathe her, put her to bed, and just play and hang out. Rosen and his wife share her care equally. Until recently, that was unusual—for any father, not just for macho guys. In fact, it's still somewhat rare.

Sharing what was once thought of as "woman's work" has changed all of Rosen's priorities. His workday is scheduled around his daughter's schedule. More importantly, he has come to realize what's really important about life.

So is Fred Rosen macho, or is he a wimp? He's definitely a tough guy who can stand up to a slimeball who's killed somebody with his bare hands. He's also a guy who puts his little girl to bed with a song from the *Barney* show.

Macho?

Nah. Just a real guy's guy.

>> Who You Are <<

Not every guy will be able to spend so much time with his baby as Fred Rosen does. Not everyone will want to. The important thing is that we can. We don't have to be chained to macho myths that don't fit anymore. That doesn't make life a bowl of cherries, of course. But it goes a long way toward removing some of the pits.

Bottom line: Who you are is up to you. Breaking the stereotypes is a real guy's thing.

<<< It's a Guy's World >>>

Web Sites

The Adolescence Directory On-Line
http://education.indiana.edu/cas/adol/adol.htm

Boys & Girls Clubs of America
http://www.bgca.org

Do Something
http://dosomething.org

GORP—Great Outdoor Recreation Pages
http://www.gorp.com/

Healthy Relationships
http://fox.nstn.ca/~healthy

Manhood Home Page
http://www.manhood.com.au

Men's Net
http://infoweb.magi.com/~mensnet

MenWeb—Men's Issues
www.vix.com/menmag/menmag.html

My Future
http://www.myfuture.com

Professor Puberty
http://www.ugcs.caltech.edu/~bh/pp

Sex, Etc.
http://www.sxetc.org/

Stop the Violence...Face the Music Society
http://www.stv.net

The Student School Change Network.
http://www.nmia.com/~sscn/

Teen Advice
http://www.teenadvice.org

Virtual Kid's Puberty 101
http://www.virtualkid.com/p101_menu.html

The Whole Family Center—Kid & Teen Center
http://www.wholefamily.com/kidteencenter/index.html

Youth Assistance Organization
http://www.youth.org/elight/

Youth in Action Network Home Page
http://www.mightymedia.com/youth

<<< Get Booked >>>

Books About Health and Physical Stuff

Bausch, William J. *Becoming a Man: Basic Information, Guidance and Attitudes on Sex for Boys.* Mystic, CT: Twenty-Third Publications, 1988.

Bourgeois, Paulette, et al, *Changes in You and Me: A Book about Puberty, Mostly for Boys.* Kansas City, MO: Andrews McMeel Publishing, 1994.

Golliher, Catherine. *Puberty and Reproduction.* Santa Cruz, CA: ETR Associates, 1996.

Madaras, Lynda, and Area Madaras. *My Body, My Self for Boys.* New York: Newmarket Press, 1995.

Slap, Dr. Gail B., and Martha M. Jablow. *Teenage Health Care.* New York: Pocket Books. 1994.

Books About Love, Sex, and Sexuality

Bauer, Marion Dane, ed. *Am I Blue?: Coming Out from the Silence.* New York: HarperCollins Children's Books, 1995.

Chandler, Kurt. *Passages of Pride: True Stories of Lesbian and Gay Teenagers.* Los Angeles: Alyson Publications, 1997.

Mastoon, Adam. *The Shared Heart: Portraits & Stories Celebrating Lesbian, Gay, & Bisexual Young People.* New York: William Morrow & Co., 1997.

Pinsky, Drew, and Adam Carolla. *The Dr. Drew and Adam Book: A Survival Guide to Life and Love.* New York: Dell Publishing, 1998.

Rench, Janice E. *Understanding Sexual Identity: a Book for Gay and Lesbian Teens and Their Families.* Minneapolis, MN: Lerner Publications., 1992.

Books About Role Models, Friends, Etc.

Ambrose, Stephen E. *Comrades: Brothers, Fathers, Heroes, Sons, Pals.* New York: Simon & Schuster, 1999.

Hinton, S.E. *The Outsiders.* New York: Puffin Books, 1997.

Peck, Lee. *Coping with Cliques.* New York: Rosen Publishing Group, 1992.

Wirths, Claudine, and Mary Bowman-Kruhm. *Your Circle of Friends.* New York: Twenty-First Century Books, 1995.

Novels About Being a Guy

Cadnum, Michael. *Edge, A Novel.* New York: Viking Children's Books, 1997.

Mazer, Harry. *Twelve Shots: Outstanding Short Stories About Guns.* New York: Delacorte Press, 1997.

McDonald, Joyce. *Swallowing Stones.* New York: Bantam Books, 1997.

Paulsen, Gary. *Hatchet.* New York: Aladdin Paperbacks, 1987.

Pinkwater, Daniel. *The Education of Robert Nifkin.* New York: Farrar, Straus & Giroux, 1998.

Randle, Kristen D. *Breaking Rank.* New York: William Morrow & Co., 1999.

Salinger, J. D. *The Catcher in the Rye.* New York: Little, Brown & Co., 1951.

Salisbury, Graham. *Shark Bait.* New York: Bantam Books, 1997.

Thomas, Rob. *Rats Saw God.* New York: Simon & Schuster, 1996.

Videos

Renting a video this weekend? Here are some old movies with a wide range of guys struggling to get it right.

American Graffiti (PG)

Breaking Away (PG)
Chariots of Fire (PG)
Dead Poets Society (PG)
Some Kind of Wonderful (PG-13)

<<< Index >>>

<<< Credits >>>

About the Author

Jeremy Roberts writes for young readers and adults. A former newspaper reporter, he has written a number of books for Rosen Publishing, including works on skydiving and climbing.

He's been a guy all his life.

Photo Credits

Cover, pp. 13, 27 by Thaddeus Harden; pp. 5, 7, 22, 24, 40 by Brian Silak; p. 10 © CORBIS/AFP; pp. 16, 20, 29 © ARTVILLE; pp. 32, 36 © CORBIS/Bettmann; p. 35 © CORBIS/Larry Lee.

Series Design and Layout

Oliver H. Rosenberg

Consulting Editor

Amy Haugesag